Riding
My Bike

Written by Anna Schlooz
Photography by Michael Curtain

sundance
A Haights Cross Communications Company

Do you see that girl learning to ride her bike?

That's me!

Do you see that girl
riding her bike
by herself?

That's me!

Do you see that girl
riding her bike
into the flowers?

That's me!

Do you see that girl riding her bike across the yard?

That's me!

Do you see that girl riding her bike through the gate?

That's me!

Do you see that girl riding her bike through the puddle?

That's me!

Do you see that girl riding her bike everywhere?

It's me!